SUPER GROSS

POOP, PUKE, AND BOOGER PROJECTS

Elsie Olson

Consulting Editor, Diane Craig, M.A./Reading Specialist

Super Sandcastle

An Imprint of Abdo Publishing
abdobooks.com

ABDOBOOKS.COM

Published by Abdo Publishing, a division of ABDO, PO Box 398166, Minneapolis, Minnesota 55439.
Copyright © 2019 by Abdo Consulting Group, Inc. International copyrights reserved in all countries.
No part of this book may be reproduced in any form without written permission from the publisher.
Super SandCastle™ is a trademark and logo of Abdo Publishing.

Printed in the United States of America, North Mankato, Minnesota

102018
012019

THIS BOOK CONTAINS RECYCLED MATERIALS

Design and Production: Mighty Media, Inc.
Editor: Megan Borgert-Spaniol
Cover Photographs: Mighty Media, Inc.; Shutterstock
Interior Photographs: iStockphoto; Mighty Media, Inc.; Shutterstock

The following manufacturers/names appearing in this book are trademarks: Anchor®, Argo®, Chef Boyardee®, Elmer's®, FloraCraft®, Gedney®, Hershey's®, Knox®, Market Pantry®, Mom's Best Cereals®, Mott's®, Nestle®, Texas Instruments

Library of Congress Control Number: 2018948866

Publisher's Cataloging-in-Publication Data
Names: Olson, Elsie, author.
Title: Super gross poop, puke, and booger projects / by Elsie Olson.
Description: Minneapolis, Minnesota : Abdo Publishing, 2019 | Series: Super simple super gross science
Identifiers: ISBN 9781532117329 (lib. bdg.) | ISBN 9781532170188 (ebook)
Subjects: LCSH: Gastrointestinal gas--Juvenile literature. | Excrement--Juvenile literature. | Science--Experiments--Juvenile literature. | Science--Methodology--Juvenile literature.
Classification: DDC 507.8--dc23

Super SandCastle™ books are created by a team of professional educators, reading specialists, and content developers around five essential components—phonemic awareness, phonics, vocabulary, text comprehension, and fluency—to assist young readers as they develop reading skills and strategies and increase their general knowledge. All books are written, reviewed, and leveled for guided reading and early reading intervention programs for use in shared, guided, and independent reading and writing activities to support a balanced approach to literacy instruction.

TO ADULT HELPERS

The projects in this title are fun and simple. There are just a few things to remember to keep kids safe. Some projects require the use of sharp or hot objects or nuts. Also, kids may be using messy materials such as glue or paint. Make sure they protect their clothes and work surfaces. Review the projects before starting, and be ready to assist when necessary.

KEY SYMBOLS

Watch for these warning symbols in this book. Here is what they mean.

HOT!
You will be working with something hot. Get help!

NUTS!
This recipe includes nuts. Find out whether anyone you are serving has a nut allergy.

SHARP!
You will be working with a sharp object. Get help!

CONTENTS

SUPER GROSS!

There are tons of super gross things in the world. These things can make you feel **disgust**. But did you know this feeling can keep you safe? It stops you from touching or eating things that might be harmful.

Disgusting things can still be fun to think about. That's why many people are **fascinated** by gross things. And poop, puke, and boogers can be especially gross!

GROSS POOP, PUKE, AND BOOGERS

Your body produces all kinds of gross **substances**. Poop, puke, and boogers are just a few examples. They might seem **disgusting**, but they all serve an important purpose. They help your body get rid of substances it doesn't need. Some of these substances can even harm you!

ALL ABOUT POOP, PUKE, AND BOOGERS

POOP

After a meal, your food takes a trip through your **digestive** system. This is the part of your body that breaks down the food you eat. Your body takes in the **nutrients** you need to survive. Any leftover waste is turned into poop.

PUKE

The food you eat usually moves from your stomach into your intestine. But sometimes your stomach pushes the food back up and out of your mouth. This can happen if there is a virus or harmful bacteria in your body. Your body tries to get rid of these **germs** by puking.

BOOGERS

Your nose is full of **mucus**. This slippery **substance** traps dust, bacteria, and other matter you breathe into your nose. Mucus keeps this matter from entering your lungs. Sometimes mucus dries out to form clumps called boogers!

MATERIALS

COCOA POWDER

BIRDSEED

SUGAR SPRINKLES

CRACKERS

POLYSTYRENE BEADS

CORN SYRUP

NYLON STOCKING

VINEGAR

MIXED NUTS

CORNSTARCH

8

POWDERED MILK

CANNED RAVIOLI

GLITTER AND GLITTER GLUE

APPLESAUCE

PEANUT BUTTER

INSTANT OATMEAL

QUICK OATS

UNFLAVORED GELATIN POWDER

BORAX

CHOCOLATE CHIPS

DINOSAUR TURD

Mix up and bake a pile of ancient dino poop!

MATERIALS 🔥

- large bowl
- measuring cups
- flour
- salt
- cornstarch
- spoon
- water
- baking sheet
- pebbles, sand, or rice
- brown and green paint
- paintbrush

1. In a large bowl, stir together 2 cups of flour, 2 cups of salt, and 1⅓ cups of cornstarch.

2. Stir 1⅓ cups of warm water into the mixture. Then knead the mixture until a thick dough forms.

3. Place the dough onto a baking sheet. Shape it so it looks like a giant piece of poop. Push pebbles, sand, or rice into the dough to create a bumpy **texture**.

4. Preheat the oven to 350 degrees Fahrenheit (177ºC). Bake the dough for ten minutes, then let it cool.

5. Mix the brown and green paints together to make a gross color. Paint the poop and let it dry.

11

SWEET BOOGER SNACK

Create supersweet edible boogers that look disgusting!

MATERIALS 🔥

- measuring cups
- water
- mixing bowl
- 3 packets of unflavored gelatin powder
- spoon
- green food coloring
- corn syrup
- sugar sprinkles
- tissue

1. Have an adult boil ½ cup of water and pour it into the bowl. Stir in the packets of gelatin powder.

2. Stir in several drops of food coloring. Then let the bowl sit in the refrigerator for at least five minutes.

3. Slowly add ½ cup of corn syrup to the gelatin mixture.

4. Stir sugar sprinkles into the mixture until the mixture gets clumpy.

5. Use your hands to break the mixture apart into booger-shaped clumps.

6. Pull several boogers out onto a tissue for a sweet but sickening display.

13

FAKE PUKE PILE

Make fake **vomit** that looks disgustingly real!

MATERIALS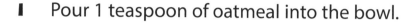

- measuring cups and spoons
- instant oatmeal
- mixing bowl
- spoon
- applesauce
- 1 packet of unflavored gelatin powder
- cocoa powder
- colorful cereal
- water
- baking sheet
- waxed paper

1   Pour 1 teaspoon of oatmeal into the bowl.

2   Stir in ⅓ cup of applesauce and the gelatin powder.

③   Add 1 teaspoon of cocoa powder and 2 tablespoons of cereal to the bowl.

④   Have an adult boil some water. Then stir 2 tablespoons of hot water into the mixture.

5   Allow the mixture to cool for about five minutes.

⑥   Cover a baking sheet with waxed paper. Pour the mixture onto the waxed paper. Use a spoon to shape the pile to look like **vomit**!

POOPY PLATTER

Model your **digestive** system to make your own poop!

MATERIALS

- canned ravioli
- 1 sleeve of crackers
- mixing bowl
- measuring spoons
- water
- fork
- blender
- vinegar
- nylon stocking
- scissors
- binder clip
- baking sheet
- spoon
- plate

1. Pour the ravioli and crackers into the mixing bowl.

2. Add 6 tablespoons of water to the mixture. This should be just enough water to get the food wet.

3. Mash the mixture together with a fork.

4. Pour the mixture into a blender.

5. Add 2 tablespoons of vinegar to the blender.

6. Blend the mixture on low until it is smooth. Add more water if the mixture is too thick to blend.

Continued on the next page.

7 Cut a nickel-size hole in the stocking's toe. Fold the toe up and clip it with a binder clip.

8 The next few steps are messy, so do them over a baking sheet and roll up your sleeves! Spoon the mixture into the stocking, gently shaking it down toward the toe as you go.

9 Position the stocking over a plate and remove the binder clip.

10 Squeeze the stocking gently from the top down, so the mixture comes out of the toe of the stocking and onto the plate. Make poop shapes on the plate!

Grossed Out! From Pasta to Poop

Mouth (Steps 1–3): In your mouth (mixing bowl), the pasta mixes with saliva (water). Your teeth (the fork) mash the pasta into smaller pieces that are easier to swallow. The pasta moves down your esophagus into your stomach.

Stomach (Steps 4–6): In your stomach (blender), the pasta mixes with stomach acid (vinegar). This breaks down the pasta. From there, the food moves to your intestine.

Intestine (Steps 8–9): Your small intestine (top of stocking) absorbs the pasta's nutrients. Anything leftover is waste. This moves to your large intestine (bottom of stocking). The large intestine absorbs extra water and turns the waste into solid poop.

Rectum (Step 10): The rectum is the very bottom of your large intestine (toe of stocking). It pushes the poop out of your body.

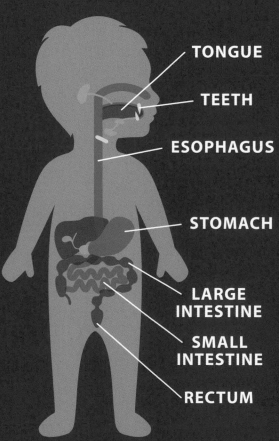

TONGUE

TEETH

ESOPHAGUS

STOMACH

LARGE INTESTINE

SMALL INTESTINE

RECTUM

FAIRY PRINCESS PUKE

Create glittery puke fit for a princess!

MATERIALS 🔥

- measuring cups and spoons
- water
- craft glue
- mixing bowls
- spoons
- food coloring
- glitter
- borax
- polystyrene beads
- non-latex gloves

1 Stir together ¼ cup of water and ¼ cup of craft glue in a small bowl.

2 Add several drops of food coloring to make a purple or pink color.

3 Add 3 tablespoons of glitter to the glue mixture.

Continued on the next page.

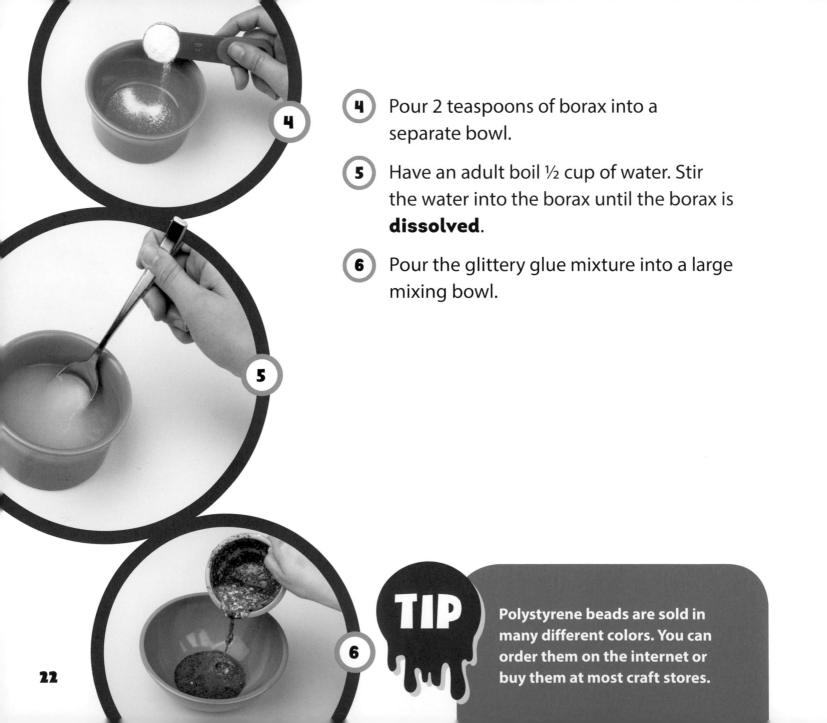

4 Pour 2 teaspoons of borax into a separate bowl.

5 Have an adult boil ½ cup of water. Stir the water into the borax until the borax is **dissolved**.

6 Pour the glittery glue mixture into a large mixing bowl.

TIP

Polystyrene beads are sold in many different colors. You can order them on the internet or buy them at most craft stores.

7. Add the borax mixture to the large bowl.

8. Add 2 cups of polystyrene beads to the bowl.

9. Put on the gloves. Knead the mixture together with your hands. Add more food coloring and glitter as needed.

BIRD POOP ART

Use foods that birds really eat to make a poop-inspired painting!

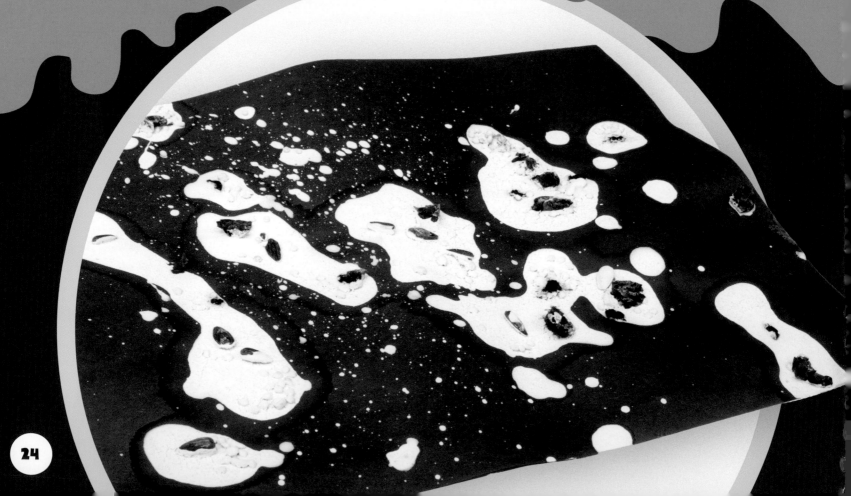

MATERIALS

- squeezable bottle with cap
- white paint
- measuring spoons
- birdseed
- dried berries
- water
- black construction paper

1   Fill the squeezable bottle about a quarter full with paint.

2   Add several teaspoons of birdseed to the bottle.

3   Tear some berries into small pieces that can fit through the bottle cap's opening. Add the pieces to the bottle.

4   Add a few tablespoons of water to the bottle.

5   Twist the cap onto the bottle and shake the bottle to mix everything together.

6   Open the bottle cap and squirt the bottle contents onto the construction paper. Let the paper dry. Your work of art should look just like bird poop!

NO-BAKE SCAT SWEETS

These snacks look just like animal turds, but they taste delicious!

MATERIALS

- mixed nuts
- cutting board
- sharp knife
- baking sheet
- waxed paper

- measuring cups and spoons
- powdered milk
- cocoa powder
- sugar
- salt

- mixing bowl
- spoon
- peanut butter
- water
- quick oats
- chocolate chips

1 With an adult's help, chop two handfuls of nuts into smaller chunks. Set them aside.

2 Cover a baking sheet with waxed paper.

3 Pour 3 tablespoons of powdered milk, 3 tablespoons of cocoa powder, ½ cup of sugar, and ¼ teaspoon of salt into a mixing bowl.

4 Stir the mixture together.

Continued on the next page.

5 Stir in ½ cup of peanut butter.

6 Have an adult boil some water. Add ½ cup of hot water to the mixture.

7 Add 1½ cups of oats to the mixture. Stir to combine everything into a thick dough.

Grossed Out!

Animal poop is known as scat. Scientists study scat to learn which wild animals are living in a certain area. Scientists look at the size and shape of scat to determine which animal it came from. They also look at matter in scat that has not been digested, such as bones, fur, seeds, or insect wings. This tells scientists what the animal has eaten!

8. Stir the chopped nuts and ½ cup of chocolate chips into the dough.

9. Scoop balls of the dough onto the waxed paper. Use your hands to shape the dough balls to look like animal scat.

10. Allow the dough to cool and harden in the freezer for at least ten minutes. Then gobble up these tasty turds!

BOOGER FAKE-OUT

These sparkly, sticky boogers are the perfect gag to gross out your friends and family!

MATERIALS

- measuring cups and spoons
- borax
- mixing bowls
- water
- mixing spoons
- green glitter glue

(**1**) Pour 2 tablespoons of borax into a bowl. Stir in 1 cup of water until the borax is **dissolved**.

(**2**) Pour 2 tablespoons of glitter glue into a second bowl. Stir in 3 tablespoons of water.

(**3**) Add 2 teaspoons of the borax **solution** to the glue mixture. Stir the mixture until it thickens.

(**4**) Take a piece of the mixture and roll it between your fingers to make a booger. Repeat this step to make other boogers.

(**5**) Smear the boogers on door handles, tables, school supplies, and other objects to gross out your friends and family!

GLOSSARY

absorb – to soak up or take in.

digestive – relating to digesting. To digest is to break down food so the body can use it.

disgust – a strong feeling of dislike toward something unpleasant or offensive. Something that gives the feeling of disgust is described as disgusting.

dissolve – to become part of a liquid.

edible – safe to eat.

esophagus – the tube that carries food from the throat to the stomach.

fascinate – to interest or charm.

germ – a tiny, living organism that can make people sick.

mucus – a slippery, sticky substance produced by the body.

nutrients – something that helps living things grow. Vitamins, minerals, and proteins are nutrients.

solution – a mixture in which a solid, liquid, or gas has become part of a liquid.

substance – anything that takes up space, such as a solid object or a liquid.

texture – what something feels like, such as rough, smooth, hard, or soft.

vomit – the stomach contents that come out of the mouth when a person throws up.